HOW TO RAISE F

Complete guide to Caring, Health, Diet,
Breeding, Habitat and tips on how to raise
Healthy Fiber Goats

DR. OWEN LIZZY

Table of Contents

3

CHAPTER ONE

INTRODUCTION

Fiber goats are a great hobby or art that can also be a source of income. Why are fiber goats so special to you? You may be surprised to learn that fiber goats are responsible for some of the most sought after fibers, such as cashmere or mohair. You're likely to have been shocked if you've ever touched or worn a cashmere sweater. Most people say "luxurious" and "smooth" or even "silky". It's no wonder that so many people want it. It's a high-end product that can be considered sophisticated, comparable to caviar or diamonds.

Mohair is a luxurious and sought-after fiber that can be used to make sweaters, socks, and other clothing. Fiber goats are highly sought-after, it's no surprise. You can start right now if you are interested in learning how to create a profitable fiber goat business or if you are an artist/hobbyist who would like to grow cashmere and mohair to use for your home spinning.

These strategies can be used to breed, produce and sell.

Start By Learning Fiber Goat Basics

What is a Fiber Goat?

A goat that is designated as a fiber goat can produce cashmere and mohair fibers from its fleece. A fiber goat is sometimes called a hair goat.

What uses is goat fiber?

Mohair is coarse with long fibers. It's used to knit garments. Because the fibers of cashmere are shorter, they can be used to make woven clothes.

What is Mohair?

Mohair is derived from the Arabic mukhayyar meaning choose or choice. It is the fabric or yarn made from Angora goat. It is known as "The Diamond Fiber", and is considered a luxurious product, similar to silk or cashmere. It is soft and silky, and can be mixed with other textiles to create garments like scarves, scarves, gloves, blankets, and carpets.

What is Cashmere?

Cashmere is a goat fiber that has a soft and downy winter undercoat. The fiber must meet specific specifications to be considered "cashmere". It is harvested when the goats start to molt in Spring. The undercoat naturally separates and creates a pocket of air. The surface hairs (called guard hairs) are then removed from the undercoat. Cashmere clothes are 8x warmer than woolen clothes, despite being lighter. It is a premium product because of this and the fact it is soft and not scratchy.

TERMINOLOGY OF FIBER GOAT

Angora goat - This breed produces mohair.

Angora wool - A textile that is derived Angora rabbits. This wool is not made from goats. Mohair, Cashmere, and Cashgora are the only fibers from goats.

Cashgora – A goat fiber quality that falls somewhere between the Angora and Cashmere types. **Cashgora-** type goats are sometimes called Cashgora goats. They are usually a cross between Cashmere goats and Angora goats.

Cashmere- A textile that is made from any goat with enough quality, downy winter undercoat. Cashmere is a luxurious item because of its warmth and softness.

Fiber Goat – A broad term that refers to any goat that produces mohair, cashmere (a variety of breeds we will discuss below), or Cashgora from

Angora goats crossed with cashmere goats.

Goat Fiber- Fiber is the material made from goat hair that is mohair, cashmere, or cashgora. There are many stages to fiber.

Raw- (combed from the goat before any processing).

Processing- (has had been dehaired and washed).

Virgin- (fiber made from fibers that have been used in yarns or products the first time).

Recycled- (Fibers made from scraps or fabrics.

Guard hairs- This is the hair that grows through the subcoat and remains all year after it is combed or molted.

Mohair – The silky and fleece made from the long hairs of the Angora sheep. Mohair can be used to make yarn and fabric. Mohair comes from the Arabic Mukhaya, which means cloth made of brightly lustrous goat hair.

Learn about Fiber Goat Breeds

Which are the best fiber goats?

Mohair goats, also known as Angora Goats, are a popular breed of fiber goat. Cashmere goats are another popular fiber goat breed. A Cashmere goat, however, is not a goat breed. It is a group of goats that produce cashmere fibers. Cashmere fibers can be gathered from a variety of goat breeds. These are collectively called Cashmere goats. Crosses between Cashmere goats, Angora goats and other goat breeds are another popular breed of fiber goat. Examples include the Pygora and Nigora breeds. Let's look at the history of these fiber goats and their characteristics.

FIBRE GOATS HISTORY

Angora Goats

Angoras are a very ancient breed. Their existence can be traced back as far as the Paleolithic period of history in the region of Ankara, Asia Minor. They are likely to be a direct descendant of the Central Asian Markour (Capra Falconeri) wild goat. The 14th century BC contains actual records about the use of Angora goathair. These are some interesting facts about the history and evolution of the Angora goat: In 1550, a Danish man discovered goats (now Angora) and started his own successful fiber goat business.

They were so impressive, that a pair was presented to Pope John Paul II in 1554. The popularity of Mohair grew due to the marketing efforts by the Dutchman, and the fame gained by presenting the goats to Pope Francis. The Sultan of Turkey banned the export of raw fleece, goods, and goats. This ban lasted for several centuries, until Queen Victoria succeeded in convincing Turkey to lift it. After the ban was lifted in 1830-1861, Angora goats were exported to Australia, South Africa and New

Zealand. These exports were the basis of the breed that we now know. Angoras arrived to the US in 1849. They eventually thrived in Texas, which is the third largest Mohair supplier in North America.

ANGORA GOAT CHARACTERISTICS

Mohair is produced by Angora goats. They don't produce Angora yarn. This product is only made from rabbits.

Is there Angora goat wool? No.

The fibers of sheep or the Angora Wool obtained from rabbits are called wool.

FIBER GOAT CARE AND OTHER HEALTH CONSIDERATIONS

Angora goats are more likely to have problems with their feet than sheep. This is especially true when they live on lush pastures. Diarrhea, caused by worms and infectious diseases, is common in Angora sheep. They are also more likely to contract flystrike and dermatophilosis, as well as lice, flystrike and scabby lips. Because of their thick coats, they are more vulnerable to external parasites. They aren't considered to be hardy and they are not prolific breeders. They have high nutritional needs to support rapid hair growth. Mohair will be less if you don't eat the right nutrition.

HYPOTHERMIA IN FIBER GOATS

After shearing, Angora sheep are practically naked until their coats have enough insulation to cover them. This can take several weeks. Because goats don't have the fat layer under their skin like sheep, they are more vulnerable. They are more susceptible to cold stress in windy and wet weather. A rumen that is full of food, especially roughage, generates heat, which helps to keep the animal warm. You can raise Angoras in a healthy way if you are conscious of their needs.

ANGORA CROSS GOATS

Mini Fiber Goats

Mini fiber goats can be cross between Angoras, larger dairy/meat goats and smaller breeds. Let's take a look at some examples of Angora goat cross.

Pygora Goats

Pygora is a cross between a registered Pygmy goat and an Angora goat.

Pygora Goat Origin

The Pygora goat is a new breed. They are the result of Katherine Jorgensen, an Oregon native, crossing them. In the 1980s. She wanted to create a small goat capable of producing fine fiber for hand spinning. The Pygora Breeders Association in the U.S. was founded in 1987.

Pygora Goat Facts

F1 Pygmy-Angora cross (aka F1) is not considered true Pygoras. To produce true Pygoras, these F1s should be bred with other Pygora or Angora breeds. Three types of fleece are produced by registered Pygoras (to be discussed later). Type A: mohair Type Type B: cashgora type C: cashmere.

Because they don't have to put their energy into lactation for children, pregnancy, or milk production, the wethers produce more fiber than the does. The life expectancy of Pygora goats is 12-14 years. Pygoras are primarily bred to produce fiber. However, they can also be used for dairy goats (producing about 1 litre per day). They also appear in competitions and fairs as well as 4H shows. There are no health problems that they have specific to their breed.

All goats require the same care. Pygoras can be handled easily and are very friendly. Pygoras can be found in a variety of colors, including white, brown, black or gray, as well as a mixture of all of these colors.

Nigora Goats

The Nigora is small goat breed, which is raised for both milk and fiber. It is usually the result of crossing Nigerian Dwarf bucks and Angoran does. Today's Nigora goats could also have the bloodlines from registered Swiss mini-dairy goat breeds. It is not easy to determine if a goat can be considered a Nigora.

Primarily, a Nigora goat must conform to certain specifications established by the American Nigora Goat Breeders Association.

Nigora Goat Origin

The Nigora was not even born until 1994, making it more recent than the Pygora. In 2007, the American Nigora Breeders Association (ANBA) was established.

Nigora Goat Facts

The Nigora goat is calm and a great choice as a pet. The 3 fibers they produce are the same as Pygoras, but the Nigora is primarily Type 2 Cashgora.

Nigora goats are able to tolerate all climates. They come in a variety of colors, including black, brown, red and mixed shades. The Nigora goats are very resilient. All goats require care, but Nigoras have special considerations.

CHAPTER TWO

OTHER ANGORA CROSS GOATS

An Angora can be cross with other breeds, as we have already mentioned. Many goat owners love their Angora crosses with milk or meat goats like the Alpine, Nubian, and Boer breeds. However, they report much less fiber when these crosses are used. One goat breeder reported that a cross produced 6 lbs of fiber per year, while a pure Angora produced 16.

Here are some examples of common **Angora goat cross:**

- Alpine Angora Cross Goats
- Boer Angora Cross Goats
- Nubian Angora Cross Goats

Crosses of Angora goats tend to shed their fiber. In this case, they don't need to be sheared but they also don't produce as much fiber than an Angora.

Cashmere Goats

What type of fiber does Cashmere come from?

Cashmere goats are not restricted to a specific breed of goat. They can be any goat that produces cashmere yarn fibers. Cashmere goats are known for their fine, soft and downy Winter undercoat. This undercoat should be able to produce cashmere in commercial quantities and quality.

The history of cashmere fiber goats

Although cashmere (or Pashmina), goats aren't as old as the Angora, we know that they were raised in Nepal, Kashmir, and Mongolia for many years. Cashmere's history is as varied as each breed. The soft, warm fiber of these goats, which could be extracted from their undercoat, was discovered by the rest the world over time.

Many other goat breeds have been bred to make cashmere.

Cashmere Goat Characteristics

It is impossible to list all the characteristics of cashmere goats, as there are so many breeds. Cashmere goats are sensitive to cold/wet conditions, especially after removing their undercoat. They need shelter. Cashmere goats do not belong to any particular breed. Therefore, it is important that you get specific information and care about the breed you are considering.

CASHMERE GOAT BREEDS

AUSTRALIAN CASHMERE GOAT

These goats were bred from feral goats that were brought to Australia in 17th-century Australia by Portuguese and Dutch navigators. They are medium-sized and produce both meat and milk as well as fiber. Australian cashmere goats can be hardy and easily raised, but they require constant care. They are smart and curious and less likely than other goat breeds to jump over fences. They come in a variety of colors, including black, red, tan and brown.

Spanish Meat Goats are Fiber Goats

Crossbreeding pure Spanish goats with cashmere goats has produced a dual-fiber/meat goat. While the Spanish meat goats are as strong and tough as purebreds but not as durable, cross breeds can be just like strong. Spanish meat goats can come in any color or variation of any goat.

CASHMERE MADE FROM DAIRY GOATS

Toggenburg Dairy Goats as Fiber Goats

The Toggenburg goat, a Swiss dairy goat, is the oldest known breed of dairy goat in the world. It's medium in size and has a range of colors from light brown to dark gray. They thrive in colder temperatures and are more productive in them. Toggenburgs make a wonderful choice for farms with children because they are gentle, calm, and friendly.

Saanen Dairy Goats are Fiber Goats

Saanens, a Swiss dairy goat of medium or large size with a classic white/beige hair color, are the ideal choice. They are gentle and carry themselves with dignity and grace. They thrive in colder climates, but they can adapt to warmer climates if there is enough shade. Saanens are a great starter goat breed and a good choice for children.

Nubian Dairy Goats are Fiber Goats

Nubian goats are outgoing, social goats that love humans. They are native to the Middle East, and can tolerate extremely hot climates. Nubians are large goats which produce butterfat-rich milk.

CASHMERE MADE WITH OTHER FIBER GOATS

Nigerian Dwarf Goats are originally from West Africa and were originally bred to be meat-eaters. They were transported to Europe as meat goats after being discovered by Europeans. This was especially important for large cats at zoos. Some animals were kept in zoo exhibits after they were released. A few animals ended up at Gladys Porter Zoo, Brownsville, Texas. This is where the Nigerian Dwarfs were first intentionally bred. Nigerian goats can be gentle, playful and lovable. They make great companions for children and seniors.

PYGMY GOATS AS FIBER GOATS

The Pygmy goat is a domestic goat breed that was originally from Western Africa. They were brought to Europe by British colonial rulers in the 19th century. These are small goats that can be colored in gray, brown, brown, or even black. They can be light- or dark-colored, and sometimes they mix colors with one another. Pygmy goats can be social animals. They need companions but they don't have to be the same species. They are friendly, affectionate and playful.

They are not susceptible to any health issues and can be raised in many climates. They love to jump and might be able to jump onto small vehicles. A good fence is essential.

Fun fact: They enjoy swimming in warm weather, which is rare because goats don't like to get wet. They are naturally born swimmers. They will spend their summer days in the water if they have access to it. It is important to note that most Nigerian and Pygmy goats don't produce enough fiber to make them worthwhile as cashmere goats. Many people cross these goats with

Angoras to make the Pygora and Nigora goats. They can produce the right fiber but have a smaller goat that needs less space and is easier to handle.

CHAPTER THREE

FAINTING GOATS AS FIBER GOATS

Myotonia congenita is a congenital condition that causes facial weakness in goats. They may fall over for 10-15 seconds if they're surprised by their ability to move their muscles to run or jump. They don't feel faint in any way. The condition is not muscular and doesn't affect the nervous system. They are conscious, but they can't move. It is believed that the fainting goat came from Nova Scotia to Tennessee during the 1880s. Four of the fainting goats were brought by a man, who then sold them to another person who raised them and noticed that their children also displayed the same behavior. He was determined to create a new breed. They were nearly extinct in the 1980s. However, The American Livestock Breeds Conservancy (now known as the Livestock Conservancy), placed the breed on an endangered list. Although the numbers have increased, there are still less that 10,000 of them worldwide. They are now considered rare and placed on a watchlist. They are more expensive than other goats because they are rare. They are usually between $300 and $600.

If you are looking to raise goats for fiber, it might be worth the extra cost if your climate is cold. Cashmere is a common ingredient in the diets of many fainting goats. Evidently, this breed is very productive. Fainting goats can be very hardy and don't jump or climb well. This makes them easy to handle. They are easy to care for and have an adaptable personality. They are not considered dairy goats as they don't produce any milk. Although their muscles are as stocky as meat goats, they are not usually raised for meat due to their high value in breeding and selling. We have covered several goat breeds that are suitable for use as fiber goats.

GET INVOLVED IN THE FIBER GOAT COMMUNITY

You can get involved in local, state, and national fiber goat groups to help you get started. It is a great way for you to network with other fiber goat keepers and learn from experienced ones. These associations are great resources for anything related to goat breeds, including care and feeding and production and business.

Goat Fibers

For the purpose of selling fiber, it is crucial that fiber goat farmers understand the quality of each fiber.

TYPES OF FIBER GOAT FLEECE

Type A - Mohair type Fiber

This can be either the Angora goat or a crossbreed that produces fiber with both ringlets as well as sheen. Type A fiber can be sheared. Mohair can be mixed with guard hairs, but Type A mohair is the least. To get a high-

41

quality fiber product, these hairs must be removed from all classifications. Because Mohair fiber is too fine to be machine dehaired, picking them out is best done manually.

Type B – Cashgora Fiber (mixture of Type A & Type C).

This fiber is a cross-breed goat product, such as Pygoras or Nigoras. It is only used for cottage industry yarn and by spinning craftspeople.

Type C - Cashmere

This fiber is the undercoat of a goat.

Let's take a look at the properties and qualities of goat fibers for Mohair and Cashmere.

MOHAIR FIBER PROPERTIES AND QUALITIES

Mohair is known as "The Diamond Fiber" for many reasons.

- It is luxurious and soft.
- Mohair retains heat well
- Mohair's outer scales reflect light, giving it a luster or natural glow.
- It is not flammable

- Mohair is one of the strongest animal fibers and is therefore considered to be durable.

- It is very resistant to soiling and dyes well.

- Mohair is resistant to stretching and sagging. It can stretch up to 30% of its length, and then return back to its original shape.

DIMENSIONS OF MOHAIR FIBER

Mohair fibers should be between 3 and 6 inches depending on their fineness. The average diameter of a Mohair fibre is between 25 and 45 microns. The fiber's diameter increases as the animal ages. Therefore, fleeces made from younger Angoras can be used to make fine clothing and carpets.

CASHMERE FIBER PROPERTIES AND QUALITIES

Cashmere is distinguished by several characteristics:

- Cashmere feels soft and fluffy next to your skin, and it breathes well.

- It does not have any body odor because it has natural antibacterial properties.

- Because of its hollow fibers, it will keep you warm in cold weather and cool in hot.

- It retains moisture, so you can be warm even when you are wet.

- Cashmere is naturally resistant to fire.

- It doesn't produce static.

- Cashmere can be abrasive so it is best to not wear it with coarse cloth or polyester fibers.

Dimensions of Cashmere Fiber

Cashmere fibers are typically 1.5-3 inches in length.

Cashmere strands are typically between 7 to 19 microns in diameter, with an industry average of 14 microns.

CHAPTER FOUR

EVALUATION AND JUDGING OF MOHAIR AND CASHMERE

Grading Mohair Fibers

The quality of mohair varies from one goat to another. American Society for Testing Materials has established the grades. Grades are determined primarily by fineness and length. However, there is a small amount of attention to character, condition, strength, purity, and luster. Mohair is divided into classes and grades.

Mohair Classes Based on Length

- Class A: 12-16 cm

- Class B: 10-12 cm

- Class C: 7-10 cm

Mohair grades based on fineness

- Fine

- 1/2 Blood

- 3/8 Blood

- 1/4 of the Blood

- Low 1/4 Blood

(Note: These names are for grades only and do not identify the breed of the animal.

Grades according to length:

- **Clothing -** Mohair is the longest fiber in clothing grade
- **French Combing** – A medium-fiber length that can be used to combing French combs
- **Staple -** The length of a staple is measured in inches over a 6-month period. Staple length is 6 inches for every 6 months of growth.

GRADING CASHMERE GOAT FIBERS

Cashmere's quality is judged by the fineness and length of its fibers. The Cashmere and Camel Hair Manufacturers Institute defines

Cashmere to be: "The fine (dehaired), undercoat fibers that are produced by a Cashmere sheep.

- Fiber is usually non-medullated, and its mean diameter does not exceed 19 micron.
- The co-efficient for variation around the mean should not exceed 24%
- Cashmere fibers exceeding 30 microns cannot exceed 3% by weight.

CASHMERE QUALITY GRADES

Grade A - Highest Quality

Grade A cashmere fibers are the shortest and thinnest. They measure between 14-19 microns in diameter and can reach up to 36 millimeters in length. Cashmere products made of grade A fiber have the best quality and are the most durable.

Grade B

Grade B is approximately 19 microns. This is a great grade. However, those who want the best Cashmere must choose grade A Cashmere.

Grade C

Grade C Cashmere has the lowest quality. This fiber is approximately 30 microns thick. They are cheaper than cashmere that is graded as type A or B, but can be used for carpets and heavy coats. After you are familiar with goat fibers as a product and have the knowledge to raise your own goats, the next step is to learn how to do it.

DEVELOP THE SKILLS REQUIRED TO

RAISE YOUR OWN FIBER GOATS

CHAPTER FIVE

RAISING GOATS FOR FIBER

Basic Fiber Goat Needs (common with non-fiber goats).

What space does a fiber goat need?

A rule of thumb is to have 10-15 square feet of indoor shelter/pen space per adult and 500 square feet minimum of outside pasture.

Fiber Goat Shelters

All goats should be protected from predators at all times, especially at night. Goats require shelter from the sun, rain, snow, and heavy winds.

They need to be dry. Sometimes children and adults need more space to feel secure and comfortable. All breeds can be accommodated with a minimum height at the back eave of 4-6 feet, and a minimum height at the front eave of 6-8 feet. Concrete flooring is preferred over wood as it absorbs odors. Make sure to keep the straw and bedding clean. You will need to provide shelter for your pets if you live in an area with very cold or windy conditions. Shelter can also be used to protect them. Shelter can be used to keep predators away at night. If they are not protected by an enclosure, livestock guardian dogs may be recommended.

FIBER GOAT EQUIPMENT

Fiber Goat Fencing

Goats are curious creatures that will eat whatever is available. Many breeds are agile and have been known to be escape artists. A fence that is good quality will last a lifetime, so make sure you do your research and don't cut corners. Equipment for feeding fiber goats includes:

- Storage of feed
- Food bowls and buckets
- Hay manger

- Mineral feeder
- Water buckets

Not all animals should be allowed to drink and eat at the same.

Fiber Goat Bedding Material

Pine or straw shavings are common. Avoid cedar shavings as they can cause respiratory problems.

Fiber Goat Collars

Your goats will often require collars. This allows you to hold on to your goats while you take them in for medical procedures, shearing or milking. In case your goats get their collar stuck on something, make sure they are easy to remove and put on. If you aren't around to help, a goat might strangle themselves.

Fiber Goat Leashes

When you need to take your goats to a new area or move them in and out of a trailer, leashes are a great option. Most goats are easy to leash train.

Fiber Goat Hoof Trimmers

It is very affordable to buy a good pair of hoof trimming scissors. You can try different brands to find the one that you like. Different hoof trimmers may look different.

However, one brand might wear out quickly while another brand could last years. You can watch videos to learn how you can trim the hooves of a goat. At least four times per year, your goats' hooves should be trimmed. They could develop hoof rot or other serious health issues.

HOW TO FEED FIBER GOATS

A barnyard goat will only eat alfalfa, hay and grain. This is no more than 1 cup per day for an adult and 1/2 cup per child. It's a good idea to have some land on which your goats can enjoy natural forage.

Water for Fiber Goats

Clean water is vital to goats' daily lives. It should be always available and kept clean. A goat's health is at risk if they drink contaminated water.

Minerals for Fiber Goats

Supplemental minerals are important for goats. It is a good idea to have both baking soda (for digestion), and minerals available. Copper and Selenium, which are mineral that goats might eat depending on where they live, are often lacking. It may be beneficial to supplement the goat's diet with additional sources of certain minerals if they are lacking in your region. If not addressed, mineral deficiencies can lead to serious diseases and illnesses in goats.

Fiber Goat Health Care

You must be mindful of the general health needs of goats, including good nutrition, water, fencing, shelter, and proper water supply. Make sure to learn about any health issues or weaknesses of the goat breed you are considering, and that you have a qualified vet on hand for treatment and consultation.

Basic goat care includes:

- Vaccinations

- Periodic blood tests
- You must be attentive to your goats' needs and be able observe for signs and symptoms like fatigue, muscle weakness or weight loss, weight gain, limping, difficulty breathing or mucus discharge.

HOW TO BREED FIBER GOATS

Bucks can breed at any time, except when it is extremely hot or cold. Angoras are naturally seasonal breeders. After a 150-day gestation period, the buck is introduced to the doe in the autumn. The kids are then produced the next spring. Young does (2-year olds) who are able to conceive twins after their first attempt at kidding tend to have single children. Angora goats only produce enough milk to feed their offspring. They may be weaned around 3-4 months old or left to their mothers until they are natural rebuffed. Other breeds of goat are affected by the heat seasons. Nigerians, Boers, Spanish, Fainting Goats. Pygmies, and sometimes Nubians can all breed year round. The majority of other dairy breeds are seasonal, and breed between August-January and May-October.

The does have approximately 21 days between their breeding cycles. The Angora crosses like Nigora or Pygoras have only one breeding cycle per year. Discuss with your vet the needs of your goat based on its breed or cross-breed to determine the best way to manage their reproduction.

Special Fiber Goat Products

Fiber goats are more sensitive than other goats to Copper toxicity, but less sensitive as sheep. If you are looking to start a small fiber company, goats are easier to manage than sheep. These are the specific fibers that goats need to be aware of:

- Fiber goats are more delicate and docile than other breeds.

- Sensitive to cold and wet more than other goats

- Lice infestation is more common in this population.

- Hoof trimming is more frequent than with other goats.

- Shearing Angoras twice per year is required

- Cashmere goats need to be combed once a year.

FEEDING FIBER GOATS

A fiber goat must be fed a high quality diet to ensure maximum growth of Cashmere and Mohair.

Angora goats require a high-protein diet that includes plenty of alfalfa or grain. Black Oil Sunflower Seeds (BOSS), are also good sources of fats that help to create luxurious, shiny fibers.

DISBUDDING AND DEHORNING FIBER GOATS

It is possible to disbud baby goats with some non-fiber goats in order to prevent them from growing horns. There are many reasons to not dehorn or disbud an Angora goat. First, disbudding Angora goats is against the ideal breed standards set by associations such as the American

Angora Goat Breeders Association. Horns are also important in goats that are raised for their fiber. The thick, woolly coats of the goat's horns allow for a lot more blood circulation. Horns also regulate body temperature. The goat's horns work in a similar way to a radiator for cars. They cool the engine coolant with air, and then circulate the coolant back into it to absorb more heat. Keep goats with horns can pose a danger to other goats and people. Fiber goats' horns can be "tipped" by using hoof shears and secateurs to trim the last 1 cm.

This solution is safe and keeps the horns in their temperature-regulating function.

- Some breeders of Cashmere goats claim that there are good reasons to disbudding or dehorning them.
- Safety for people
- Safety of the herd: Goats have a hierarchy, and it is not uncommon for them to butt other goats' heads.
- Horns can get caught in fences, which can lead to panic, distress, injury, or even death.

- Many shows require that you disbudded your goats in order to be safe if you are going to compete.

- Some breeders do not disbud their cashmere goats because of this. These are some of the reasons:

- Cashmere goats will grow thicker coats if they keep their horns.

- The horns regulate the body temperature and will be a great benefit to the goat.

- The horns can be used as handles for holding and handling a goat.

- The unpleasant disbudding procedure that must be done on a goat child can be avoided by keeping horns.

For milk and meat, raise fiber goats

Cashmere can be a great way to build a goat farm with multiple streams. This will allow you to create multiple income streams from fiber, milk products, and meat. This strategy allows you to build a strong foundation for a business that generates multiple income streams. After we have covered the basics of raising fiber goats, let us now discuss the next step: how to harvest valuable fibers from goats.

LEARN HOW TO HARVEST FIBER FROM A FIBER GOAT

Raw fiber from a fiber goat can be either sheared Mohair from an Angora or combed Cashmere (or cross-breed) without the guard hairs.

CHAPTER SIX

GOAT FIBER HARVESTING ALTERNATIVES

Fiber Goat Natural Seasonal Shedding

The climate determines the length of a Cashmere goat's shedding period. They shed more in winter than they do in warmer climates. This could be between March and May. You may notice shedding earlier if you live in warmer climates. Both Type B and Type C goats can shed their fibers. Angoras do not. Cashmere is best harvested without the naturally shed undercoat. It can be difficult to gather as the wool will come off in small tufts or pieces. The goats may also rub fences to remove it, which can cause damage to the fiber. You will find guard hairs and other debris.

Combing Fiber Goats

It is important that you note when your goats start to shed. This is a great time to begin removing the fiber as it releases. It is best not to begin too soon as it can be very difficult. Natural separation of the goat's undercoat helps in the combing process. It is important not to wait too much. A lot of your fleece may be lost if you see tufts along the fences. You will need several tools to pull the Cashmere through the guard hairs when you are combing. You can find many great resources online, including YouTube videos that teach you how to do it. The Cashmere can be removed easily if you have the right tools, and the right timing. Some goats even love it or fall asleep. There are many tips and tricks to separate the guard hairs from the fleece. It is important to note that "combing" occurs when the goats are removed from their fibers. This is different than the "combing", which occurs after the fibers have been processed. The first step in harvesting the fleece is to combine the raw goat fiber. The second type of "Combing", which occurs later, involves opening and seperating the clean fiber. This is one of the final steps in the process that leads to the fiber being ready to be spun.

CARDING FIBER FROM A FIBER GOAT

Carding is the act of straightening fibers in preparation for spinning. You can do carding by hand or with two wire dog brushes-shaped hand carders. A carding machine that has wires on rollers can be used to do larger-scale carding. Carding machines can be small, portable machines for personal use or large industrial machines for commercial purposes.

- Shearing Fiber Goats
- Shearing Angora Goats

Angora goats must be sheared and not combed.

- This equipment is required:
- Stand for goat shearing
- Blow dryer (for removing hay/debris before shearing).
- For trimming, use electric shears or clippers
- Shelter is a way to keep goats warm when they're sheared.

- Optional blanket for goats to wear after shearing
- Scissors
- Burlap bags, not plastic, are used to store the fiber of each goat.
- For weighing fiber, use a scale
- Mesh bags to wash fibers

The Angoras are sheared twice per year, in Spring and early autumn. The climate in your area will determine the exact length of the shearing process.

HOW TO SHEAR ANORA GOATS

Your goats should be kept dry. To keep your goats dry if it rains before shearing, you can put them in an enclosed barn. You should put them in the fridge for 24 hours before you shear. Some fiber goat breeders also provide goat coats for each goat before shearing in order to prevent them from absorbing hay or other contaminants into their fleece. Before you begin shearing, remove any debris, such as dirt, manure, and hay from the goat. You should start with the youngest goats and work your way up to the oldest. Because the youngest goats have the best and most valuable mohair. The coarser fibers of older goats shouldn't be mixed in with the finer ones. Begin at the belly and work your way up to the udder/scrotal. Next, you will need to trim the sides starting at the belly and moving onwards towards the front. Next, you will need to shear each leg of the back. Finally, trim the crown of your head from the tail to the back of the goat. To remove excess hair, use the scissors. Separate any stained, soiled or other contaminants. The unsoiled fleece should be weighed and rolled up.

Keep the fleece dry. Before the next goat arrives for shearing, make sure to sweep the area.

SHEARING CASHMERE GOATS

Many fiber goat breeders don't shear their cashmere goats as it reduces the quality and value of the fiber. This is because the coarse guard hairs are mixed with the fine cashmere. It's much harder and more time-consuming to remove guard hairs from fleece than to comb the cashmere off goat.

- Making Fleece from a Fiber Goat
- Skirting a Fleece: How can I skirt a fleece
- Skirting refers to the process of cleaning fleece and making it spinnable.

You can remove any unwanted parts of the fleece such as matted sweat locks and fiber under the legs, tail, or belly which are discolored or not good enough for spinning. The preparation and shearing are the most important steps in skirting. The fleece is then carefully rubbed to remove any Mohair or Cashmere that isn't salable quality.

Fiber Goats are a great source of fiber

Scouring refers to the washing of natural fiber contaminants like sweat and gland wax. Scouring also removes fine soil and vegetation, as well as urine, and other contaminants. Here's an example of how a Mohair fleece is usually scoured.

Use hot water. (approx. 145°F and some type detergent

The fleece should be soaked for 30 minutes in a mesh bag. Rinse it twice.

To bring out the natural shine of the fiber, add a few drops of vinegar or denatured alcohol during the final rinse.

- After washing the fleece, hang it flat in a dry area.
- For faster drying, use a fan to blow the fiber.

Fiber Goat Dehairing Process

After the fiber is sold by the breeder, dehairing is an industrial process. The remaining guard hair is removed from the fleece by dehairing machines. The machine's design allows the fleece to flow through it while the coarse hair is removed. This converts the fleece to knitting and weaving grade fiber.

Combing Fiber and Carding Goats

After scouring, the next steps are carding and combing. These are techniques to separate the strands from the lumps of washed yarn, ensuring that the yarn is smooth and high-quality. These processes open and straighten the fibers, as well as any clumps that may have formed following scouring. They also remove any vegetable matter or other material from the fiber. The tools used are the main difference between combing and carding. The tools used for carding are very similar to the fine rectangular dog brush. Combing can also straighten the fibers and align them with one another. You can use paddle combs. They are very similar to hand cardsers but only have one or two rows. These are great for working medium-to-long fibers and Cashmere. The paddle comb's straight metal teeth move slowly through the fiber. Industrial combing involves large circular machines. Combing and carding are not always necessary. Both methods straighten fibers and remove vegetable matter or contaminants.

Both align fibers in the same direction. Carding is preferable if you desire a more fluffier product.

Combing makes fleece compacter and aligns fibers better.

Dying Goat Fiber – Dyeing Mohair, Cashmere and Dyeing Goat Hair

For both Mohair or Cashmere, there are three stages at which fibers can dye. It can be dyed after scouring and is called Stock Dyed (or Fiber Dyed) for best results. It can be dyed after spinning and is called Yarn Dyed. This refers to when the fiber spools are dyed after spinning.

It is also known as Piece Dyeing if it is dyed after knitting or weaving. This is when the yarn is woven into a product like a sweater or a sweater.

HOW TO TURN CASHMERE FIBER INTO YARN

Cashmere can be very finely worked with. Cashmere should have a tight twist, or a higher tension than any other fine fiber. However, it shouldn't be too tight that it loses its soft feel. Spinning Mohair is different from spinning Cashmere. You don't want to get a very tight twist. Instead, you want as loose (or low) as possible. As long as the yarn is strong enough.

Low twist allows light bounce off of more fiber surfaces, and highlights the Mohair's luster. The yarn will be duller if it has a high twist.

CHAPTER SEVEN

Home Spun Cashmere

You can spin with either a drop spindle, or a spinning wheels. You can learn how to spin your yarn by visiting a specialty yarn shop. You can then decide if you would like to use a drop spindle, or a wheel. After we have covered how to harvest fibers from a goat fiber fiber, let's now discuss how to make a profit with those fibers.

PROFIT WITH FIBER GOATS

You should consider all the income streams your goats could produce as well as the demand and supply of goat fibers on the market if you are thinking about opening a fiber business.

Fiber goats for profit

When calculating potential profits from goats, one consideration is whether your goats can be used for multiple purposes. Many goat farmers are interested in knowing if their goats can be used for both fiber production and milk production.

Goats for fiber and milk (dual purpose)

Can angora goats milked?

Angora goats don't produce much milk so they aren't considered dairy goats. Angora doesn't typically produce enough milk to feed more than one child.

Can angora goats be used as meat?

Although Angora goats do not produce a lot meat, it is reportedly high quality enough to be marketed as a premium meat for restaurants and other high-end meat purveyors. Even so, an Angora goat's Mohair is likely to be more valuable than its potential for meat production. When assessing the potential profit from raising fiber goats, another important factor to consider is the demand for goat fibres on the market, particularly in your locality.

Current Mohair Demand

Mohair is highly in demand. According to the World Textile Information Network, Mohair is in high demand. This is due to its natural attributes and industry's commitment towards sustainability.

The University of California Small Farm Program identifies this opportunity for mohair producers: "The U.S. Government has a direct payment program for Mohair producers in order to maintain a viable industry."

Direct payments through the U.S. Department of Agriculture (USDA) Agricultural Stabilization and Conservation Service are based on the difference in the national average market prices and a support. Producers received on average $2.475 per dollar of Mohair they marketed in a recent year. You can find more information at the ASCS offices located in many countries.

If you want to get into the fiber goat industry, you need to understand not only the national demand trends for goat fibers but also the local market. Contact your local yarn/knitting/spinning guild to find out what kind of fiber they are interested in. This will allow you to get a feel for your local cottage/niche.

GOAT FIBER SALES AND PRODUCTION

Mohair Production and Marketing

Pounds of Mohair – How much wool can an Angora goat make?

An average Angora goat can produce 12-18 pounds of Mohair each year.

Mohair Price Per Pound

According to USDA statistics for 2018,

- A pound of mohair on the commercial market can be sold for as high as $7.88
- A product with more value will yield a higher return.
- For a pound of fiber, washing and preparing it for spinners can bring in up to $40.00
- The return on investment for yarn made with this fiber is up to $150.00 (USDA, 2017).

- The USDA publishes a weekly report about the National Market Price of Mohair (and Wool) on a weekly basis.

Cashmere Sales and Production

Cashmere in Demand

Cashmere is in high demand. The quality of the cashmere is exceptional (soft, light, warm, durable), but it doesn't have a lot of volume.

Cashmere Production Per Goat

According to the Agricultural Marketing Resource Center (AMRC), a Cashmere goat that is well-bred will produce approximately 4-6 ounces per year of Cashmere fiber.

Cashmere Price Per Pound

Cashmere fiber ready to be spun can sell at $25.00 an ounce, which is equivalent to $400 per pound. You will need to create a plan to start your profitable goat fiber business once you have analyzed the market for goat fiber, including local demand, supply and pricing.

Fiber

START YOUR OWN FIBER GOAT BUSINESS

Angora Goat Business Plan - Are Angora Goats Profitable?

It can be very lucrative to commercially farm Angora goats. Mohair is being used by cottage industry customers in Mohair for a variety of products. Mohair is a luxurious fiber that can be used for clothing. It is also fireproof. For example, people have started small businesses that sell Mohair baby blankets and mattress padding.

A Mohair production company has a high probability of becoming a successful business if you consider the initial investment required to raise your Angora goats.

Cashmere Goat Plan

Apart from the basic business considerations (equipment, setup, and purchase of the goats), there are also different business plans for Cashmere goats depending on the breed you choose, and whether you intend to raise them for fiber or for milk or meat. We have already mentioned the fiber goat associations as a great resource for information on starting a Cashmere goat farm. You can join any of these associations while you're setting up your equipment. Ask questions and follow the threads in their forums. Experts are available to offer sound advice and guidance.

WHERE TO BUY FIBER GOATS

It's worth looking on Craigslist, local classified ads or the livestock section for listings. Anyone can also call themselves a breeder and make a sale of goats with problems. An official recognized organization is the best source for fiber goats for sale.

You can find a list listing reliable breeders of Angora goats on the Eastern Angora Goat and Mohair Association. You can also meet reliable goat breeders at farmers markets and livestock fairs. Avoid auctions because many people will sell their "problem" goats to someone else. Cashmere goats can also be searched by breed to find the best deal.

Fiber Goats: The Price

- A dairy goat can be purchased for between $50 and $300

- For a young Pygmy goat it's $150-$400.

- Average Boer goat prices range from $80-$100
- Nigoras start at $150
- Pygoras are available in a range of $150-$500.
- Because they are rare, Fainting goats can be purchased for $300-$600

These numbers are only estimates and will vary depending on your gender, age and registration.

This guide will inspire you to consider the fiber goat business if you are looking for a lucrative opportunity and love working with animals.

It is a great time to start. The demand for high-quality mohair and cashmere is on the rise. These results in huge rewards for goat farmers who want to produce these fibers. We encourage you to try the water and purchase a few fiber goats if you are interested. They will require lots of work and time. It can be a profitable business if you start your own herd and make some marketing connections. You'll also find that you enjoy working with these relatable and entertaining animals.

THE END

Printed in Great Britain
by Amazon

21712110R10061